IMAGES
of America

CORPUS CHRISTI

CORPUS CHRISTI.

This sketch by an unknown artist portrays the encampment of Gen. (and future president) Zachary Taylor, whose so-called "Army of Occupation" made the shores of Corpus Christi Bay home between August 1845 and March 1846. Taylor eventually marched to the Rio Grande to enforce it as the southern U.S. border. Mexico considered Taylor's arrival an act of aggression and sent troops across the river. Pres. James K. Polk accused Mexico of invading U.S. soil, and on May 13, 1846, Congress declared war on Mexico. Taylor and other U.S. generals captured several cities in Mexico and finished things off by taking Mexico City. Mexico acknowledged defeat and on February 2, 1848, signed the Treaty of Guadalupe Hidalgo, which established the Rio Grande as the border between Texas and Mexico. The campsite is commemorated by a marker in Artesian Park in downtown Corpus Christi.

ON THE COVER: Mesquite Street looking north toward the old First Methodist Church shows that Corpus Christi had become somewhat of a modern city by the time this photograph was taken in 1922. Automobiles lined the streets, electrical wires crisscrossed the skies, and fire hydrants had been installed. Those appear to be trolley tracks in the middle of the street. The city's trolley system was destroyed by the 1919 hurricane but was rebuilt. By 1931, as automobiles became more common, trolleys ceased operating completely. The First Methodist Church building in the distance was located at Mesquite and Mann Streets. One of the city's most recognizable buildings, it was torn down when a new church was constructed on Shoreline Boulevard in 1955.

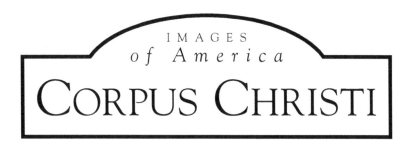

IMAGES
of America

CORPUS CHRISTI

Scott Williams

ARCADIA
PUBLISHING

Published by Arcadia Publishing
Charleston, South Carolina

Library of Congress Catalog Card Number: 2008931755

For all general information contact Arcadia Publishing at:
Telephone 843-853-2070
Fax 843-853-0044
E-mail sales@arcadiapublishing.com
For customer service and orders:
Toll-Free 1-888-313-2665

Visit us on the Internet at www.arcadiapublishing.com

*To my children, Avery and Grace, who worked very hard at letting me
have the time needed to compile this book.*

CONTENTS

ACKNOWLEDGMENTS

This book would have required oodles more work had it not been for the Corpus Christi Public Libraries, which has placed more than 11,000 historical photographs on its Web site at www.library.ci.corpus-christi.tx.us. Their digital archives make it easy to search for photographs by all sorts of criteria or browse through the collection at random. People can even request copies to be sent to their own e-mail accounts. All of the photographs in this book are from their vast collection.

I especially want to thank the staff of the Central Library's local history department, who fulfilled my numerous requests for photographs and tolerated me and my somewhat noisy scanner. Staff members who assisted me were Laura Garcia, Gerry Riojas, Taylor Hendrix, Gwen Perrenot, and Veronica Martinez.

This book would have been much more difficult to compile had it not been for the many photographs taken by John Frederick "Doc" McGregor, a Corpus Christi chiropractor who turned his love for photography into what would become a priceless archive of the city's history and culture.

I would also like to thank my editors at Arcadia Publishing for giving me this opportunity: Christine Talbot and, most especially, Kristie Kelly, who put up with my repeated mistakes and missed deadlines (although only by a few days). I'll do better next time.

INTRODUCTION

Sometime in recent history, Corpus Christi earned the nickname of "Sparkling City by the Sea," and although some parts of the city do not exactly sparkle, there are times when sunlight glinting off of Corpus Christi Bay or downtown lights blinking in the distance makes this moniker an apt description for the state's eighth-largest city.

Its history goes back to 1839 when a businessman by the name of Col. Henry L. Kinney purchased land for a trading post from the former commandant of Fort Lipantitlan, established by the Spanish in 1734, located 25 miles west of what is now Corpus Christi. Kinney faced numerous challenges from Native American raids, Texas cattle thieves, and Mexican troops, who suspected him of harboring "border pirates." But persistence paid off, and by 1846, the Texas Legislature authorized the formation of Nueces County. A year later Corpus Christi was selected as the county seat despite the fact that it would be six more years before it incorporated.

In 1850, a census of the county reported 689 people living in 151 buildings, although there were no schools or churches. More than half of the residents had been born in Mexico while only 53 had been born in Texas. In 1852, the town incorporated and residents chose B. F. Neal to serve as mayor. A yellow fever epidemic put the skids on growth in 1854. Those who survived placed their efforts on improving the city, forming a school, and establishing churches of the Catholic, Methodist, Presbyterian, and Episcopalian faiths.

Texans owned slaves, so when the Civil War broke out the Texas Legislature voted to secede from the Union, with Corpus Christi residents for the most part supporting the decision. The city did not play a significant role in the war. Union ships fired on the city at one point and occupied the town for six months, but its location on the South Texas coast placed it far away from the center of the conflict.

After the war, Corpus Christi found itself as a shipping point for Texas cattle moving to eastern markets and for crops—especially cotton, which came to be the mainstay of the region's agricultural economy. In 1874, a channel 8 feet in depth was dredged through Corpus Christi Bay, which was deep enough to welcome steamships to the city. Toward the end of the century, the city formed a fire department and acquired a daily newspaper, a hospital, and a water system. The Texas Legislature formed the Corpus Christi Independent School District in 1909, and automobiles and trolley cars replaced horses on city streets.

The first causeway linking the city with other parts of the area was built in 1911, named the Nueces Bay Causeway. It connected the city to the north with towns such as Portland, Aransas Pass, Port Aransas, and Rockport to name a few. Natural gas, electricity, and paved streets brought modern amenities to the city around 1912, and tourists began visiting Corpus Christi for its warm weather and beaches.

Hurricanes have played a big role in the city's history and culture. Major storms hit the city in 1916 and 1919. The 1916 hurricane destroyed the aforementioned causeway, ravaged the bay front, and killed 20 people. The 1919 hurricane proved even worse, devastating the city and killing 287 people. At this point, city residents decided they needed two things more than anything else: a seawall to protect them from storms and a deepwater port to bolster the economy.

Achieving these two goals was arguably the two most critical factors in the city's survival and subsequent growth. The port and an oil boom brought enormous prosperity to Corpus Christi. In 1935, Nueces County reported 60 oil wells in two oil fields. Two years later, the number had jumped to 894 wells in 15 fields. The city's population grew from 27,742 in 1930 to 57,301 in 1940.

In 1929, the League of United Latin American Citizens (LULAC) formed to promote civil rights for Hispanics. It has grown into a national organization along with another civil-rights organization, the American GI Forum, formed by Dr. Hector P. Garcia to help Hispanic war veterans get the benefits they had earned.

Other significant accomplishments in the early part of the century included establishing a community college, opening a hospital for handicapped children, and constructing a cathedral to serve the Catholic community. The military came to town in 1938 when the U.S. Navy built Naval Air Station Corpus Christi to train pilots for the upcoming war.

In the next two decades, the city's major accomplishments included construction of a children's hospital, formation of a university, and the opening of the Intracoastal Waterway between Corpus Christi and Brownsville, which allowed barge traffic to carry cargo to and from the cities. The city built another causeway linking the mainland with Padre Island, and construction of the Harbor Bridge over the Corpus Christi Ship Channel made movement easier for both automobiles and ships.

The Corpus Christi International Airport was dedicated in the 1950s as was the Corpus Christi Army Depot, which became the largest helicopter repair facility in the world. The city annexed the Flour Bluff area, and in 1962, Pres. John F. Kennedy signed a bill authorizing the creation of Padre Island National Seashore, preserving this pristine environment for generations to come.

Interstate Highway 37 connected the city with San Antonio, and the Bayfront Arts and Sciences Park brought museums, a playhouse, a convention center, and an auditorium to the city's shores. Downtown development picked up with construction of several high-rise hotels and office buildings, most notably the twin towers of One Shoreline Plaza, which more than anything gives the Corpus Christi bay front its characteristic look.

The city began to diversify its economy in the 1980s with a new emphasis on tourism. The Texas State Aquarium and the USS *Lexington*, a decommissioned aircraft carrier turned museum, led the way. In recent years, an auditorium large enough to attract big-name performers has been added to the city's attractions, along with a baseball field to house the city's minor-league baseball team.

Through the years, growth has been slow in Corpus Christi, and while that might upset some it also protects the city from devastating economic crashes that plague faster-growing cities. The refineries and chemical plants along the Port of Corpus Christi and other areas continue to provide most of the jobs in the city, and efforts are under way to secure those jobs and create more in the future.

Longtime Corpus Christi residents enjoy the mild winters, a beautiful bay front, relaxed living, and a mixture of American and Mexican cultures that give this city its laid-back attitude and distinct bicultural flavor.

One

PRELUDE TO PARADISE
1839–1899

Henry L. Kinney is regarded as the founder of Corpus Christi. Kinney established a trading post in 1839 on land purchased from the former commander of a nearby fort. It was named Kinney's Trading Post or "Kinney's Ranch." In 1846, the Texas Legislature authorized the formation of Nueces County, and a year later (six years before it incorporated as a city) Corpus Christi became the county seat. Kinney spent much of his life touting the city's benefits. In 1848, he advertised the town in the nation's leading newspapers and did the same with many in Europe. In 1850, he hosted the Lone Star Fair and brought a carnival from New Orleans. Kinney was shot and killed in 1862 in Matamoros, Mexico.

Battalion of Artillery— --------- —8ᵗʰInfantry — 2ⁿᵈDragoons - 7ᵗʰInf. ⁵ᵗʰInf. Light Artillery — 3ᵈInf. — 4ᵗʰInfantry — Town.
1ˢᵗBrigade   2ⁿᵈBrigade   3ᵈ Brigade
GENˡ WORTH   COL. TWIGGS   LᵗCOL MᶜINTOSH   COL. WHISTLER.

BIRDS EYE VIEW OF THE CAMP OF THE ARMY OF OCCUPATION,

near CORPUS CHRISTI, TEXAS, as in October 1845

This lithograph, dated October 1845, offers an aerial view of Zachary Taylor's army. His Army of Occupation brought an estimated 4,000 troops to the small town of approximately 100 people. Imagination likely played a large role in this painting's perspective—the area around Corpus Christi is generally flat.

This is John Steward McGregor with his wife, Mary, and their daughters. The McGregors came from England in 1852, landing in Galveston on Christmas day. They settled on Turkey Creek in Nueces County on land purchased from Henry L. Kinney's agent in Europe. This is a reprint copy of an original framed photograph. (Photograph by John Frederick "Doc" McGregor.)

Mesquite Street (west side) from near Aubrey looking north to Belden

Corpus Christi has had several county courthouses through the years. This photograph shows the first and second versions located on Mesquite Street. Felix A. Blucher, one of the city's earliest settlers, designed the first courthouse on the left, while Rudolf Hollub is credited with designing and building the second courthouse on the right. Construction on the first courthouse began in 1853, while the second courthouse was completed in 1875.

This is Mesquite Street looking southwest toward the bluff sometime in the late 1800s. Writing on the back of this photograph indicates that one of the houses on the bluff is the Kenedy mansion. Mifflin Kenedy partnered with Richard King in the 1860s to begin ranching in South Texas. The two men later went their separate ways. Kenedy is said to have been the first South Texas rancher to build a fence around his land to prevent cattle rustling.

The Battle of Corpus Christi was waged on August 18, 1862. This sketch by artist Thomas Noakes shows a fleet of federal ships under the direction of Lt. John Kittredge bombarding the city as Confederate soldiers battle back. Corpus Christi citizens had chosen secession by a vote of 142 to 42.

The Frank and Weil General Store at the corner of Chaparral and Lawrence Streets is shown in this reprint of a photograph taken in the 1870s. Other buildings pictured include George Robert's Saloon, the Steen Hotel, David Hirsch (a wool dealer), the Cahill House, and the Conrad Meuly home.

This 1884 photograph shows what Corpus Christi looked like from the shoreline. The houses in the distance were situated on a bluff overlooking the bay. The bluff, which overlooks downtown Corpus Christi, offered protection from surging storm waters that inundated structures below. Nothing, however, could protect these stately homes from the ravages of hurricane winds exceeding 100 miles per hour.

This photograph of early-day surveyors was taken in 1876 and depicts Charles Blucher (back row, right) with, from left to right, (first row) brother George Blucher, Phillip Fullerton, and Hilario Martinez; (second row) brother Richard Blucher and Grove Crafts. Charles Blucher followed his father, Felix, into the surveying business. Felix Blucher, the first surveyor in Nueces County, is credited with designing the county's first courthouse.

W. S. Rankin Grocery was located on the corner of Mesquite and Peoples Streets in the McCampbell Building. This reprint is from an earlier image taken in the 1880s. Mesquite and Peoples Streets were among the earliest named thoroughfares in Corpus Christi and both still bear their original names.

Paved roads were nonexistent in the 1880s when this photograph was taken of the intersection of Carancahua and Winnebago Streets. The church steeple in the background is believed to be that of St. Patrick's Catholic Church. The city's founder, Henry L. Kinney, named the two streets after Native American tribes.

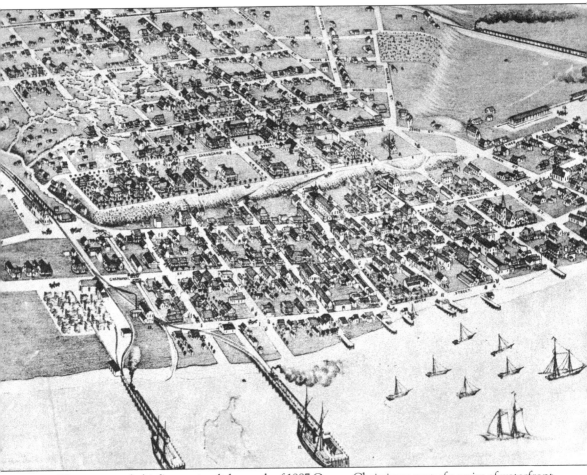

This reprint of a bird's-eye-view lithograph of 1887 Corpus Christi was part of a series of waterfront maps created by Augustus Koch. Koch was born in Birnbaum, Germany, and lived in Wisconsin and Illinois. He traveled to more than 20 states, including the far West and Texas.

The Good Shepherd Episcopal Church stands at the corner of Chaparral and Taylor Streets in this c. 1889 photograph. Writing on the back reads, "Looking eastward down Taylor St. at Chaparral. Episcopal Church faces east on near corner; Royall Givens home faces west on opposite corner."

A funeral procession makes its way down Waco Street in this 1890s photograph. Two horses, draped for the occasion, pull the funeral carriage. Embalming caught on quickly in urban areas in the late 1800s and early 1900s. Before that, funerals were held very soon after death before the body could begin to decompose.

Mrs. A. R. Brookman and an unidentified man ride in an 1890 automobile with two equally unidentified dogs. Early automobiles were nothing more than horse carriages fitted with internal combustion engines. This version appears to have been steered by the lever the man his holding in his left hand.

This is a view of downtown Corpus Christi taken in 1890 from the bluff looking east toward the bay. With construction of the seawall still many years away, the city was vulnerable to the wind and waves delivered by tropical storms and hurricanes. Weather forecasting was still in its infancy, which meant residents had little warning of approaching storms.

Several stately homes line the bluff overlooking Corpus Christi and the bay. This area is now known as the uptown portion of downtown Corpus Christi. This view looks west toward the bluff. These homes were either destroyed by hurricanes or torn down to make way for progress.

Fifth-grade schoolchildren and their teacher stand in front of the schoolhouse in this 1894 photograph. The building in the background looks very much like Corpus Christi's Central High School, which was constructed in the 1890s and was replaced with a newer building in 1911. Students attended another school on Staples Street while the new school was under construction.

Fr. Pedro Verdaguer, a native of Spain, succeeded Fr. Dominic Manucy as bishop of the region that included Corpus Christi. He died on October 26, 1911, while on a confirmation tour near Mercedes, Texas. His body was brought back to Corpus Christi and a requiem high mass was offered for him at St. Patrick's Church on Sunday, November 1, 1911.

This photograph, taken in 1890 at the corner of Chaparral and Peoples Streets, depicts several mule teams loaded with iron casing to be used in building artesian wells on the King Ranch southwest of Corpus Christi. These wells provided a more reliable source of water. W. S. Rankin Grocery (right) and Corpus Christi National Bank (second to the right) are featured in many historical photographs.

Unidentified members of the Bluff City baseball team sit for this team photograph in 1892. A caption under the original photograph states that the team "defeated [a] combined team from Princeton and Harvard Universities." Another local team, the Corpus Christi Kids, who played around the turn of the century, was also touted as having excellent talent.

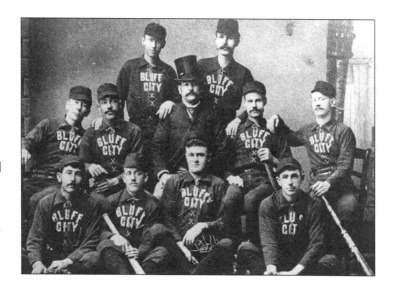

This is an 1890s view of downtown Corpus Christi looking northeast from the bluff. The city progressed rapidly in the 1880s and 1890s. Many city streets were paved for the first time, a street railway system began operating in 1889, and a public water system began in 1893.

This group of residents makes the most of a rare snowfall in 1897 by pelting each other with snowballs in front of the Bidwell Hotel on Mesquite Street. Snow is a rare sight in Corpus Christi and the rest of South Texas. It is so rare, in fact, that many residents have never seen it other than in photographs.

Two

RISING FROM THE DUST
1900–1925

This view from sometime around 1910 or before is of the west side of Chaparral Street looking south from Schatzel Street. Streetcar tracks run down the street in front of several downtown businesses, including Saddle-Rock Restaurant. The trolley at this time might have been powered by mules since there are no power lines visible above the street. The first electric trolley line began service in 1910 via the Corpus Christi and Interurban Railway. Various owners struggled to make a profit with the trolley system. The line lost money until Camp Scurry, an army training post located in what is now the Del Mar neighborhood, opened in 1916. In less than a year, the number of riders exceeded one million and the future of the trolley business looked bright, until the 1919 storm severely damaged both the track and the trolley cars. Repairs brought the trolley system back into operation by November 1919. The trolley system survived the storm, but it could not survive the onslaught of the automobile, and by 1931, trolleys ceased operating in Corpus Christi for good.

An unidentified woman waits in a railroad ticket office with a ticket office employee in this 1911 photograph. The calendar above the woman's head and the one on the wall in the back of the office suggest the image was snapped on August 8. As the sign above the woman's head states, tickets for the Pullman Company's sleeper cars also were available. By 1911, Pullman held a monopoly on sleeper cars and at its peak accommodated 26 million passengers a year.

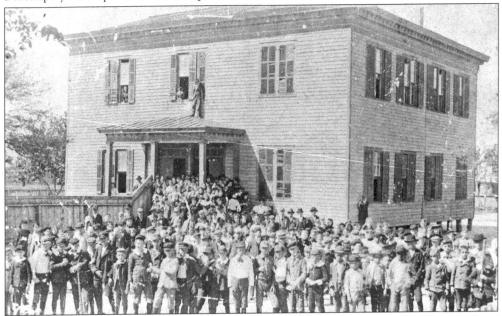

Students from Corpus Christi's Central High School, built in the 1890s, pour out into the schoolyard in this c. 1900 photograph. Although it was called a high school, many of the students look to be in elementary and middle school. A new school was constructed on this same site in 1911.

24

A parade of elephants marches down Chaparral Street sometime in 1900. It is hard to imagine a parade like this taking place in modern times now that liability issues have taken center stage. Female spectators wore long skirts and hats despite the apparent heat. Some carried parasols to shade themselves from the sun. The elephants must have felt right at home.

The *Daily Herald* newspaper staff poses in front of its office building on Mesquite Street in 1907. The people pictured are employees and delivery boys. The *Daily Herald* competed with another local newspaper, the *Corpus Christi Caller*, which published its first edition in 1883. In the 1920s, the *Corpus Christi Caller* and another newspaper, the *Corpus Christi Times*, merged.

Central Wharf, Corpus Christi, Tex.

Corpus Christi's Central Wharf ran from William Street to Laguna Street (later renamed Sartain Street). The wharf was used to unload shipments, and other photographs and sketches show sailing ships docked next to it. Another wharf north of Central Wharf was located at the end of Lawrence Street.

This postcard depicts a ship moored just north of Central Wharf. A note on the back of this postcard reads, "Three masted schooner on left, Noakes, Bros, 1904, off downtown CC, with a north wind. This is probably the ship used by Ed Cline and others to haul coral rock from Baffin Bay to Port Aransas, Corpus Christi and even to Point Isabel."

Postmarked July 30, 1909, this postcard shows the residence of Henrietta M. King, wife of the founder of the King Ranch, which eventually grew to cover 825,000 South Texas acres. Henrietta King played a major role in education in Kingsville, donating land for the first high school and working with the architect on its design.

Members of the Sinton Ladies Club don their best for this 1910 photograph. One of the women, identified on the back of the image as Miss Lizzie McGloin (back row, second from left), may well have been a descendant of James McGloin, an *empresario* who received a land grant from Mexico in 1828 to colonize 200 Irish families.

27

Epworth-By-The-Sea, also known as Epworth Inn, was located on North Beach, which is now known as Corpus Christi Beach. It was likely destroyed by the 1919 hurricane. The grounds in front of the inn, known as the Epworth League Grounds, hosted public events.

This is the Seaside Pavilion Hotel, located at the end of Taylor Street, before the 1916 storm damaged it and the 1919 storm destroyed it. A note on the back of this photograph states, "Notes from Eric Warren, Austin, Dec. 1971: Pavilion Hotel with sail scows anchored off Lone Star Fish Company wharf on extreme right. Looking east from the Pavilion wharf."

This postcard depicts Corpus Christi High School as it appeared in 1911 shortly after it was constructed. The building later became Northside Junior High School. A note on the back of the card reads, "Image shows the exterior of the High School when there was a park in front."

The writing on the back of this image states, "One of the first airplanes to arrive in Corpus Christi. It arrived here in 1912." In the background may be the pier leading to the Pavilion Hotel. Corpus Christi built its first airport in 1928 shortly after Charles Lindbergh flew over Port Aransas on a "goodwill hop" from Washington, D.C., to Mexico City. City officials speculated that Lindbergh would have landed in Corpus Christi had there been an airport.

These four men from left to right are an unidentified pilot; Edwin G. Crabbe, Corpus Christi postmaster; W. G. Blake, secretary of the Corpus Christi Commercial Club; and Eli T. Merriman, publisher of the *Corpus Christi Caller*. The photograph is dated March 29, 1913, and although no other information is available, it appears it was taken in connection with the beginning of a crude form of airmail service to the city.

Episcopal Church and Parsonage.
CORPUS CHRISTI, Texas.

This hand-colored postcard published by Corpus Christi Book and Stationary is postmarked July 9, 1912. It is addressed to "Mrs. Charles A. Meuly / Moody Hotel / Hot Springs, Arkansas." Perhaps it is just a coincidence, but the last name of "Meuly" crops up from time to time in other historical photographs in Corpus Christi. This Episcopal church on Taylor Street was located across the street from a house where former Confederates took a new oath of allegiance to the Union.

A crowd gathers in and along the street as riders on horseback, some dressed as Native Americans, assemble for some sort of public performance to celebrate the Fourth of July. The writing on the front reads, "Indians waiting for Columbus to land—July 4, 1912."

Men transfer watermelons from a wagon to what appears to be a freight car in this 1912 photograph taken in Sandia. Spanish for "watermelon," Sandia received its name from Fennell Dibrell and Max Starcke, who founded the town in 1907. They chose the name because of the large number of watermelons grown in the area.

Cars decorated for some sort of parade line Laguna Street between Chaparral and Mesquite Streets in this c. 1912 photograph. The structure in the distance is Centennial House, a historical home that is still standing today. Writing on the back states, "Conley's Cleaning and Pressing establishment was wiped out by the 1919 hurricane. The building at left is probably Belden's old warehouse."

Mexican Kitchen, Corpus Christi, Texas.

This image was used on a postcard dated 1913. It was postmarked in Goliad and was addressed to someone in Germany. Although not as well chronicled as the Anglo population, Hispanics, especially those of Mexican descent, have been a part of the Corpus Christi culture since the 1800s.

T 102. Home, Sweet Home. Mexican Jackal. Corpus Christi, Texas.

This somewhat condescending postcard shows a small home owned by a Corpus Christi resident of Mexican descent. A jacal, also spelled "jackal," was a building found throughout parts of the southwestern United States and Mexico. They were used by Native Americans before European colonization and later used by both Hispanic and Anglo settlers.

Nueces County officials pose in this 1914 photograph. County judge Walter Timon (first row, center) served in the Texas Legislature before running for the position of county judge. As president of the Corpus Christi Chamber of Commerce in 1919, Timon pushed for construction of the seawall and breakwaters as well as an extra-wide boulevard to run the length of the seawall now known as Shoreline Boulevard.

This photograph of members of the Corpus Christi Police Department shows at least four members armed with billy clubs, a weapon that originated among London police officers in Victorian England. They are about a foot long and are used to impart less-than-lethal force.

City leaders pushed for construction of the Nueces Hotel because they believed a luxury hotel was needed to attracted business and tourists. Completed in 1913, it stood six stories tall, had 230 rooms, and charged guests "$1 per day and up," according to information mentioned on the back of the postcard. It stood on the block between Water Street and Chaparral Street with its main entrance on Peoples Street. It was demolished in 1971.

Hotel Showing Corpus Christi Bay in Background, Corpus Christi, Texas.

These are members of Boy Scout Troop No. 1 in 1915. One of the scouts (back row, third from the right) is McIver Furman, who became the Corpus Christi region's first Eagle Scout. As an adult, Furman worked as a physician, founded Driscoll Children's Hospital, and served as mayor of Corpus Christi.

Camp John Paul Jones served as a training camp for the Junior Naval Reserves. This photograph is from a c. 1916 booklet published on the organization. Cadets stand in formation in front of the Corpus Beach Hotel.

The soldiers were stationed at Camp Scurry when this photograph was taken in 1916. Camp Scurry was located in what is now the Del Mar subdivision. The Fifth Engineers and Fourth Field Artillery of the U.S. Army trained here after the nation entered World War 1. The camp was an economic boon to the city.

Members of the National Guard Military Police of World War I pose in front of the Confederate Fountain in front of the bluff that overlooks downtown and the bay front. First Presbyterian Church is in the background. This is either a bad exposure or it was a very foggy day when this photograph was taken.

A piece of paper attached to this *c.* 1918 photograph describes the building as "Old Country Club House on North Beach." This is not to be confused with the Corpus Christi Country Club, which was established in 1922. This structure may have been associated with the city's first golf course, which was located on North Beach (now Corpus Christi Beach) and was destroyed by the 1919 hurricane.

Several automobiles move down the 1300 block of Chaparral Street dodging telephone poles and assessing the damage after the 1916 hurricane. This photograph is dated August 18, 1916. The hurricane (they were not named in those days) struck south of Corpus Christi on August 18 and is now estimated to have been a Category 4 storm on the Saffir-Simpson Scale, the strongest to hit the Texas coast since the 1900 hurricane hit Galveston.

The 1916 hurricane turned wooden structures into piles of mismatched lumber as seen in this photograph of the Hardin Cottages. Tropical storm–force winds of 64 to 70 miles per hour were reported as the storm neared land, and a gust of 90 miles per hour was reported as the hurricane made landfall. Rainfall totals were estimated at 1.58 inches, and the storm damaged some measuring equipment at the National Weather Service.

The Fox Cottages on the corner of Water and Power Streets were destroyed by the 1916 hurricane. Offshore, a fishing boat sank, drowning all of its crew, and on land five people died, including two who perished when a house collapsed. The storm destroyed several wharfs and numerous salt cedars.

The 1919 storm destroyed much of Corpus Christi Beach and the rest of the Corpus Christi bay front. The caption on the back of this photograph states, "Spohn Hospital in distance looking north. Our house was just this side of sanitarium. Hall's Bayou on South." North Beach was rebuilt after this storm and another Spohn Hospital sits on the Corpus Christi bay front to this day, although not on Corpus Christi Beach.

Company B poses for a group photograph in front of the Corpus Beach Hotel in 1916. These young cadets attended Camp John Paul Jones as part of their Junior Naval Reserves training. This image comes from a booklet published about the camp.

lences on Furman Avenue.   CORPUS CHRISTI, Texas.

Many of the residences on Furman Avenue depicted in this 1920s postcard are still standing today. The neighborhood, however, has declined considerably since this card was postmarked on September 28, 1920. It is addressed to Mr. Charles Von Blucher of Corpus Christi, Texas, and states, "Dear Papa: We surely were glad to get your letter. I hope you will be able to get in tomorrow or Sunday. We are going to take Nick to the bay with us in a little while for a swim. Wonder if he will enjoy it." It is signed, "Lovingly, Marie."

Schatzel and Peoples Streets, looking east from the bluff, are depicted in this postcard postmarked August 13, 1920. It is addressed to Mr. Cecil James of Burnet, Texas, and reads, "Dear Uncle Cecil, Sister and I are in Corpus and have been all week. We are having a fine time. The fish are not biting very well, but we got enough to have all we want. Cotton is fine, some make over a bale per acre. Come to see us. Write."

Schatzel and Peoples Street, east from Bluff, Corpus Christi, Texas.

This is a postcard of downtown Corpus Christi as it appeared in 1922. The 1914 Nueces County Courthouse is in the distance to the left of the photograph, while First Methodist Church is the round building in the middle. It was located at the corner of Mesquite and Mann Streets. Unfortunately this unique structure was torn down when a new church was built on Shoreline Boulevard in 1955.

Snowfall on December 20, 1924, brought this woman and four children outside to enjoy this rare South Texas experience. The boy who is seated appears to be atop a homemade sled that lacks runners. The absence of hills in Corpus Christi makes for even tougher sledding. Historical photographs always describe these events as "snowstorms," although people from more northern climes might describe this as a light dusting of snow.

The Nueces Bay Causeway connecting Corpus Christi to Portland to the north included a small segment that could be lifted to allow boats to go under it. The train on the right is traveling on the San Antonio and Aransas Pass trestle. The 1919 hurricane destroyed the causeway, and the train trestle no longer exists. This card is postmarked August 5, 1924.

Two men and a boy are on board an old fishing boat in this 1920s photograph. The Corpus Christi area, and especially nearby Port Aransas, is known as a great place for sportfishing. Corpus Christi and Aransas Pass are also the commercial fishing headquarters of the area, and the city is a seafood-processing center. Commercial shrimping has played a role in the area's economy and culture for many decades, although the industry has suffered from overseas imports.

A Corpus Christi contingent of postal workers poses outside the federal building in 1924. Postmaster Owen D. Holleman is at the far left. Others are identified as, from left to right, (seated) F. J. Jenkins, Don M. Harris, H. J. Stevens, I. C. Kerridge, W. L. DeRoche, and Joe M. Dunlap; (standing) Charles Kaler, J. F. Herold, R. L. Harrell, J. B. Pitman, E. T. Cox, and Cyrus Tilloson.

The Ku Klux Klan and others attend a funeral for W. F. "Wildfire" Johnston at Rose Hill Cemetery on June 2, 1925. Johnston ran for sheriff in 1922. The KKK, formed in Pulaski, Tennessee, in 1866, spread to Texas in March 1868. The Klan largely disappeared after the federal Ku Klux Klan Act of 1871 allowed the president of the United States to suspend the writ of habeas corpus in cases of secret conspiracy. The Klan made a resurgence in Texas after World War I.

What appears to be a couple of customers stand inside the Missouri Pacific Railway ticket office at 422 Peoples Street in the 1920s. Daily passenger train service began in Corpus Christi in 1880 and ended in 1962. Several railroads served the city throughout the years.

The Order of Sons of America (OSA) Local Council No. 4 poses on the steps of First Methodist Church at the corner of Mesquite and Mann Streets. Those identified include Ben Garza, Ernie Barrera, Lee Campbell, Juan Carrizales, Antonio Arsuaga, John Barnard, and Eulalio Mann. The OSA was one of the first statewide Mexican American civil-rights organizations, having been founded in San Antonio in 1921. The Corpus Christi council fought for a new Mexican school, the Cheston L. Heath School, which was dedicated on September 13, 1925.

Three

USHERING IN PROSPERITY
1926–1937

The Port of Corpus Christi officially opened on September 14, 1926. Two destroyers, the *Hatfield* and the *John D. Edwards*, arrived in Corpus Christi to commemorate the event. Congress authorized the U.S. Army Corps of Engineers to construct a channel 25 feet deep and 200 feet wide from the Gulf of Mexico through the jetties at Port Aransas to a point on the shoreline of Corpus Christi Bay at the mouth of a shallow bayou. Dredging began in January 1925 and ended a year later. Corpus Christi was chosen as the site for the port over Rockport, Port Aransas, or Aransas Pass because it was less susceptible to storm surges and was served by three railroads. The bluff overlooking Corpus Christi Bay is the highest point on tidewater between Veracruz and Miami.

Members of the Nueces County Sheriff's Department display confiscated distillery equipment used to make bootleg liquor. The event, chronicled in this April 27, 1932, photograph, occurred not long before Prohibition came to an end on December 5, 1933, when the 18th Amendment outlawing the sale, manufacture, and transportation of alcohol for consumption was repealed with ratification of the 21st Amendment. (Photograph by John Frederick "Doc" McGregor.)

The destroyer USS *Borie* steams into the Port of Corpus Christi as part of the opening-day celebration for this deepwater port, which opened on September 14, 1926. The Bascule Bridge was an engineering marvel for its time. The word *bascule* is French for "see-saw," an apparent description of the up-and-down movement of the bridge. Eventually the Bascule Bridge was replaced by the Harbor Bridge, allowing automobile traffic to cross the Corpus Christi Ship Channel without interruption.

Daughters of the American Revolution held a dedication ceremony for a monument marking the site where Gen. Zachary Taylor (later a U.S. president) and his Army of Occupation camped between August 1845 and March 1946 during the Mexican-American War. The marker was placed on the site of the David Hirsch School. Members pictured include Mary Carroll, superintendent of schools, and Freeman Martin, principal of the David Hirsch School. (Photograph by John Frederick "Doc" McGregor.)

Zackie's Play House Restaurant, at 509 South Water Street, attracts a large crowd attended to by uniformed female carhops. Other buildings identified in this July 8, 1939, photograph include the Civic Center in the background to the left of the drive-in restaurant and the Church of the Good Shepherd, located on the bluff in the background. (Courtesy John Frederick "Doc" McGregor.")

This is an aerial view of the Port of Corpus Christi taken on September 1, 1937, showing the port's inner harbor. Note the Bascule Bridge instead of the Harbor Bridge and the lack of a seawall, which was completed in 1940. The ships at the bottom of the photograph appear to be oil tankers, while the vessels lined up on the opposite side are most likely cargo ships. (Courtesy John Frederick "Doc" McGregor.")

The USS *Constitution*, known affectionately as "Old Ironsides," is anchored in Corpus Christi Bay. The historic warship visited the city in February 1932, remaining here for nine days. An estimated 100,000 people visited the frigate during its stay. The ship scraped the side of the Bascule Bridge entrance, yet another reason why the bridge eventually was replaced. (Courtesy John Frederick "Doc" McGregor.")

In this April 1936 photograph, a woman identified as Señora Chana shows one of the original barns at a historic colony in San Patricio, an area just northwest of Corpus Christi. The San Patricio Colony came into existence after *empresarios* John McMullen and James McGloin contracted with the government of Mexico in 1828 to settle 200 Irish Catholic families.

Boards ripped from buildings are piled up around area tourist cottages after a storm. This photograph, taken on December 14, 1934, shows how much work is left to be done following a storm that hit on September 5, 1933. In recent years, Corpus Christi has been spared a direct hit by a hurricane. (Courtesy John Frederick "Doc" McGregor.")

A toddler stands next to an early model automobile in this summer of 1928 photograph. The car is parked on the old Don Patricio Causeway, which linked Padre Island with the mainland. A car's wheels would fit inside the grooves. Note that there is only room for cars to go in one direction.

A group of Corpus Christi's Spanish-American War veterans gathers in front of a building used as a headquarters for the organization. This often forgotten war started on April 25, 1898, when the United States declared war on Spain following the sinking of the battleship *Maine* in Havana harbor on February 15, 1898. The war ended with the signing of the Treaty of Paris on December 10, 1898, with Spain losing control of Cuba, Puerto Rico, the Philippines, and Guam.

I. C. Kerridge and Frank McCaughn lead the Boy Scout Bugle and Drum Corps in a 1928 Robstown parade. The Corpus Christi Council of Boy Scouts started in 1919 with seven troops consisting of 161 scouts. The name of the Corpus Christi Council was changed in 1924 to the Nueces Valley Council. In 1928, the council's area was expanded to include Nueces County and seven other counties.

First Class

Spohn Hospital Nursing School graduates
1930
Ernestine Meyer; Catherine Harrod (McCarty); Katherine M. Smith
vis Moore (Mew); Augusta M Looney; Dr. Redmond.   (McCaleb)
Eva Bondig (Hamilton)

These are the first graduates of the Spohn School of Nursing in 1930. The school opened in 1926, and students were housed in Spohn Hospital. Dr. Henry Redmond (front row, center), dean of the school, offered his former home on Broadway to the hospital, which moved it to the hospital grounds so nursing students could enjoy a comfortable home life while attending school.

Henry Pomeroy "Roy" Miller, looking larger than life, campaigns on behalf of John Nance "Cactus Jack" Garner IV, who served as the 44th speaker of the House of Representatives and the 32nd vice president of the United States. Garner ran for the Democratic nomination for president in 1932. Miller was elected mayor in 1913 at the age of 29. He is credited with bringing a waterworks, a storm and sanitary sewer system, a garbage incinerator, electric lights, and paved streets to Corpus Christi. He also lobbied Washington for a deepwater port.

Leopard Street, seen here on August 29, 1931, is packed with vehicles and pedestrians that flocked to the area on Saturdays to shop. The downtown district of Leopard Street looks a lot different today than it did back then. It is a mixture of high-rise buildings that are closed on weekends. A few historic buildings remain a few blocks west of the bluff.

This bus, No. 13, was one of three built on a Chevrolet chassis by the Nueces Railway Company in 1930; the other two were Nos. 11 and 12. No. 14 was added the next year. These buses heralded the end of streetcars in Corpus Christi. The remaining 11 streetcars were retired on February 1, 1931.

Corpus Christi High School opened in 1929, replacing the previous incarnation that opened in 1911. The 1931 graduating class is shown here with the faculty in the rear. This was the last year the graduating girls wore white dresses and carried bouquets of roses. (Photograph by John Frederick "Doc" McGregor.)

This 1931 aerial photograph shows Corpus Christi High School (right of center) not long after it opened and the Holy Cross Cemetery (bottom right). The high school was located between Lipan and Leopard Streets before Interstate Highway 37 had been built. This image was given to Corpus Christi Public Libraries by Mary Carroll, the only woman to have served as superintendent of the local schools (1922–1933). (Photograph by John Frederick "Doc" McGregor.)

Members of the Robstown Home Demonstration Club gather for this 1931 photograph. In 1912, home demonstration work began in Texas in an effort to organize rural girls and teach them homemaking and social skills. The program was modeled after federally initiated agriculture demonstrations that had been helping Texas farmers since 1903. The national Smith-Lever Act of 1914 provided a legal base and financial support for demonstration work. (Photograph by John Frederick "Doc" McGregor.)

The steamship *Nicaragua* sank on the shores of Padre Island on October 16, 1912, after getting caught in a storm while traveling from Tampico to Port Arthur. This photograph was taken in 1932. No one knew what had happened to the ship until 10 days after it sank when several members of the crew turned up in Port Aransas in a small boat and were rescued by crew members from the U.S. Coast Guard lifeboat station. Other crew members headed south and walked 54 miles to Port Isabel. Others, who were too sick to travel and thus took shelter inside the *Nicaragua*, were rescued several days later.

Mrs. Frank de Garmo, Mrs. Sam Rankin, and an unidentified woman stand in front of the World War I Memorial cannon in the Gold Star Court of Honor between Upper and Lower Broadway near the Corpus Christi Cathedral. Mrs. De Garmo, born Mary Eloise Donnell in Covington, Kentucky, in 1865, moved to Corpus Christi around 1912 with her husband and two children. She instigated construction of this memorial as well as the Centennial Museum in South Bluff Park, which closed long ago. De Garmo also started the Memory Gardens located behind Spohn Hospital. (Photograph by John Frederick "Doc" McGregor.)

A submarine visited Port Aransas and sits in the harbor area on April 29, 1932, just across from Cowan Machine Shop. Notice that the phone number on the roof of the shop only has three numbers, a testament to the town's tiny population. In less than a decade, submarines like this would be pressed into service to defend the nation after a Japanese attack on Pearl Harbor forced the United States into World War II. (Photograph by John Frederick "Doc" McGregor.)

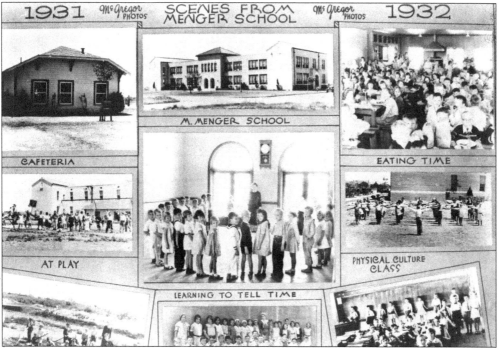

Menger Elementary School, at 2401 South Alameda Street, is depicted in these photographs taken during the 1931–1932 school year. (Photograph by John Frederick "Doc" McGregor.)

The USS *Constitution*, known as "Old Ironsides," passes under the raised Bascule Bridge that was eventually replaced by the Harbor Bridge. The ship visited Corpus Christi on February 23, 1932. Launched in 1797, the *Constitution* earned its nickname during a battle with the British ship HMS *Guerriere* in 1812, when cannonballs reportedly bounced off the ship's thick oak hull.

Four men pose next to an old car after a successful hunt that resulted in at least two bucks and a couple of strings of ducks. This photograph was taken on December 28, 1933. (Photograph by John Frederick "Doc" McGregor.)

A hurricane that hit Corpus Christi in 1933 left the ground in the Cole Park area covered in standing water. That year was the second most active Atlantic hurricane season on record, with 21 storms forming in the northwest Atlantic Ocean. The storm made landfall in Brownsville on September 5. The hurricane damaged boats in Corpus Christi, created inland cuts along the coast, and destroyed the causeway connecting Padre Island to the mainland. (Photograph by John Frederick "Doc" McGregor.)

An unidentified beauty contestant stands on the running board of an automobile, accompanied by a woman and a young girl. Bathing beauty contests were common at the time. One of the first in Corpus Christi was held in conjunction with Splash Days, which later evolved into Buccaneer Days, an annual celebration still in existence. (Photograph by John Frederick "Doc" McGregor.)

Irma and Ed McGloin, descendents of *empresario* James McGloin who brought Irish Catholic settlers to the region in 1828, demonstrate a common means of transportation used before the automobile began dominating the roads. This photograph was taken in April 1936. James McGloin emigrated from the town of Castlegal, County Sligo, Ireland, where five generations had lived and farmed.

A *c.* 1939 aerial view of the Corpus Christi bay front shows what the area looked like before the T-heads and L-head were added to the bay front. The bluff dividing uptown from downtown is visible. Interstate Highway 37 had not yet been built when this photograph was taken.

La Retama Public Library served as the city's library for many years beginning in 1915 when La Retama Club gave a "silver tea" to raise money for the cause. The first library was located at the Lovenskiold Building at the corner of Mesquite and Peoples Streets. The library survived a fire, lack of public support, and a hurricane. It had a transient existence for many years, moving from place to place for various reasons. The library was housed in the former W. W. Jones home (pictured here) from 1937 to 1955. (Photograph by John Frederick "Doc" McGregor.)

In the 1930s, North Beach was a popular destination for residents. They packed the boardwalk at a time when traveling to the barrier islands was a lot harder and took a lot longer. Ladies wore dresses, while men wore slacks and long-sleeved shirts; both genders wore hats. The boardwalk was eventually destroyed by a storm.

Corpus Christi built its first airport in 1928 and is pictured here in 1937. Voters passed a $50,000 bond issue to purchase 180 acres off Old Brownsville Road, and it began with a hangar, business office, and shell runway. Aviator Cliff Maus is believed to have been the first person to land an airplane at the new field before the runway was even completed. Regular passenger service began in 1929, and airmail service commenced in 1932. Maus served as airport manager from 1930 to 1934 when he left to take a job with Braniff Airways. He died soon after when his plane crashed in a thick fog outside Fort Worth.

A person could get a T-bone steak for 35¢ when this photograph was taken in 1934. Writing on the back states that it was taken by an "itinerant" photographer who visited the city in February of that year. The NRA sign refers to the National Recovery Administration, which came into existence in 1933. The NRA attempted to boost industry by raising wages, reducing work hours, and controlling competition. The U.S. Supreme Court ruled the NRA unconstitutional in 1935.

The Ritz Theatre, at 715 North Chaparral Street, opened for business on Christmas day in 1929. The first show was *It's a Great Life*, a Metro-Goldwyn-Mayer production. St. Louis architect Scott Dunn designed the building, which he described as an "image of fantasy" created by using art deco and Spanish Renaissance influences. The elaborate interior seated 1,300 people and featured a Spanish courtyard facade and illuminated sky. Moving clouds were projected from two cloud machines mounted on turrets near the ceiling, and stars twinkled in the sky. (Photograph by John Frederick "Doc" McGregor.)

A group of trucks loaded with harvested cotton demonstrate how important this crop has been to the region, especially in the latter half of the 19th century and the early part of the 20th century. Nueces County produced 1,010 bales of cotton in 1889. By 1910, that figure had grown to 8,566, and by 1930, the county was among the leading cotton-producing counties in the state with 148,442 bales produced. This photograph was taken on August 12, 1936. (Photograph by John Frederick "Doc" McGregor.)

The staff of the *Corpus Christi Caller-Times* poses for a group photograph in 1937. This appears to be the news reporting staff and not the entire *Caller-Times* staff. The *Caller*, which started publishing in 1883, merged with the *Times* in the late 1920s. The building that houses the newspaper was constructed in 1935 at 820 North Lower Broadway and has been remodeled several times. A $10 million press was added in 1994, and in 1995 the first Internet edition of the paper went online. The Scripps-Howard group purchased the newspaper in 1997. (Photograph by John Frederick "Doc" McGregor.)

The Nueces Transportation Company served the Corpus Christi area in the 1930s. A note on the back of this photograph reads, "Corpus Christi Bus—Fare 5 cents, 1937." The company began operating around 1933 when Bob and Ed Ekstrom purchased 13 buses from Central Power and Light on October 13, 1933. The business was located at 1317 Gavilan Street.

The Port of Corpus Christi was a successful venture from the very beginning. Near the end of cotton season, ships loading cotton as well as vessels loading lead from Mexican smelters in Monterrey often were docked two abreast. The port opened with four cargo docks. By 1928, it asked residents to issue an additional $1.5 million in bonds to build two more cargo docks. The discovery of large oil fields in San Patricio, Nueces, and neighboring counties led to the building of oil docks, and refineries began to locate along the port.

Pres. Franklin D. Roosevelt and his fishing party display a tarpon caught off of Port Aransas on May 4, 1937. Port Aransas was once renowned for the availability of tarpon, and a historic inn in the town is named for the popular game fish. One wall of the Tarpon Inn is covered with tarpon scales autographed by guests who stayed at the inn. FDR's autographed tarpon scale is on the wall, although Roosevelt stayed on a yacht during his trip to Port Aransas. (Photograph by John Frederick "Doc" McGregor.)

Four

THE MILITARY COMES MARCHING IN
1938–1961

John Ball Harney (left), who served as Nueces County sheriff from 1939 to 1953, stands with Judge Walter Timon, who served in various political capacities. After working in the Texas Legislature, Timon was the Nueces County judge from approximately 1907 to 1917, when Texas governor James E. Ferguson appointed him to the 28th District Criminal Court. His appointment came despite having been tried on voter manipulation charges in 1915 (the jury could not reach a decision in his case) and having shot his nephew, who was allegedly stalking him after a family dispute over a will, in 1916. This photograph was taken in the 1940s.

Although there is nothing on the original photograph to indicate as such, these Corpus Christi Junior College students appear to be part of a newspaper staff working (or pretending to work) on the next edition of the college newspaper. The college was established in 1935 under control of the board of trustees of the Corpus Christi Independent School District. The school's name was changed to Del Mar College in 1948. This photograph was taken in the late 1930s. (Photograph by John Frederick "Doc" McGregor.)

The writing on the back of this October 26, 1938, photograph describes these gentlemen as a "group interested in navigation and the port." The seven men posing aboard the ship presumably docked in the Port of Corpus Christi. They are identified as, from left to right, (first row) W. W. Jones, a prominent rancher and businessman; U.S. Representative J. J. Mansfield of Palacios; Richard King of the King Ranch family; and John Kellum of Robstown; (second row) Roy Miller, Corpus Christi mayor; Col. L. M. Adams; and unidentified. (Photograph by John Frederick "Doc" McGregor.)

Corpus Christi and the rest of South Texas owes much of its existence to the ranching industry. Between 1800 and the end of the Spanish dominion over the area, much of what is now Nueces County was granted to ranching families. At first, farming played a small role in the area's economy and culture, but by 1860 things had begun to change. A few large ranches still exist in the area, but it is difficult to make a living off of raising cattle. Thus some of the ranches have begun branching out into ecotourism.

Barney Farley of Port Aransas, described as a "fishing guide de luxe," officially opens the 1938 tarpon rodeo on August 17 of that year. Farley served as a guide to Franklin D. Roosevelt when he fished for tarpon in Port Aransas waters in 1937. The tarpon rodeo, despite its name for a sport on land, was a fishing tournament built around this popular game fish that once packed Coastal Bend waters. Tarpon rodeos were popular along the Texas coast until the 1950s, when the sport died. Some say the fish went away (or were overfished), while others think anglers simply lost interest. Tarpon made a comeback in the 1970s and can still be found in local waters. (Photograph by John Frederick "Doc" McGregor.)

This June 17, 1938, postcard shows the city hall building at Peoples and Mesquite Streets. The view is looking east down Peoples Street with city hall in the right foreground. La Retama Library, the predecessor to the Corpus Christi Public Library, was housed in this building at one time. The Greyhound bus terminal is across the street. (Photograph by John Frederick "Doc" McGregor.)

A railcar loaded with metal drums filled with liquid chlorine sits outside this Southern Alkali Corporation site on March 14, 1938. Southern Alkali was the first major industry to locate in Corpus Christi, taking advantage of the Port of Corpus Christi and the city's access to rail. The company later became known as Pittsburg Plate Glass. It produced chlorine and soda ash by using oyster shells. The company's arrival sparked more interest in the area from refineries and chemical plants. (Photograph by John Frederick "Doc" McGregor.)

In the early 1930s, large oil fields were discovered in the area, and the need to ship this oil led to construction of oil docks and the arrival of oil tankers. Refineries began to locate along the Port of Corpus Christi, and ships from all over the world began delivering crude oil to the port and picking up gasoline and other refinery products. (Photograph by John Frederick "Doc" McGregor.)

Several members of the Corpus Christi Fire Department pose with a fire truck parked in front of the Palace Theater on November 30, 1939. It began in 1871 as a volunteer fire department called the Pioneer Hose Company No. 1. The name was changed in 1914 to the Corpus Christi Fire Department. (Photograph by John Frederick "Doc" McGregor.)

Here members of the Nueces County Sheriff's Department gather at a local restaurant on September 15, 1938. The first sheriff of Nueces County was H. W. Berry in 1846, when the county was first organized. According to the sheriff's department Web site, it is not known who was serving as sheriff when this 1938 photograph was taken. It is also unknown as to who was fighting crime when this photograph was taken. (Photograph by John Frederick "Doc" McGregor.)

The Corpus Christi High School Buccaneers football team is shown here in September 1939. Corpus Christi High School was renamed Roy Miller High School in 1950 to honor the former mayor. Known now as the "Battlin' Buccaneers," they won the state championship in 1938 and 1960. (Photograph by John Frederick "Doc" McGregor.)

74

A handful of customers enjoy a meal at the Faust Café located at 412 North Chaparral Street on January 10, 1939. The café was located on the ground floor of the nine-story Medical-Professional Building. Another historical photograph taken in 1928 shows the Faust Café in what appears to be another block of Chaparral Street. (Photograph by John Frederick "Doc" McGregor.)

Four carhops and one other employee (or owner) of the High Hat Drive-In, at 502 South Staples Street, pose outside the small hole-in-the-wall establishment on April 15, 1939. Carhops became common in the 1940s as the popularity of drive-ins increased. Another historical photograph taken a year later shows carhops in short skirts, and the menu posted on the outside of the building reveals that patrons could purchase a fried-chicken dinner for 35¢ and a beef sandwich, cheeseburger, or goose liver for 15¢. Records do not indicate why anyone would actually want to eat a goose's liver.

Dick Flores (right), described in this June 23, 1939, photograph as "Ben Garza Park zoo keeper," displays a live alligator captured in the Hillcrest area of Corpus Christi. Although not commonly found within city limits, South Texas does have a few places where alligators can make their homes. Two such sites are Lake Corpus Christi, northwest of the city, and the Aransas National Wildlife Refuge, which is due north. (Photograph by John Frederick "Doc" McGregor.)

Born in the pre–Civil War days, minstrel shows featured white performers who blackened their faces with burnt cork or greasepaint. One of the stock characters in these performances was named Jim Crow, whose name came to describe a complex system of laws and customs in the South that were used by white Americans to maintain an oppressive culture over African Americans. In this 1939 photograph, taken at the Lions Club Minstrel Show, the cast gathers for the grand finale of this performance held at the Ritz Theatre. Joe Roscoe, a businessman, real estate developer, and in this instance director of the show, is at the top center of the photograph. Minstrel shows died out during the 1950s as African Americans began to campaign for civil rights.

Clara Driscoll and W. A. Wakefield Jr. led a grant march at the celebration of the birthday of Pres. Franklin D. Roosevelt at the Plaza Hotel deck. This photograph is dated January 31, 1940, but Roosevelt was actually born on January 30, 1882. (Photograph by John Frederick "Doc" McGregor.)

Members of the Mexican American Chamber of Commerce meet with Mexican consul Javier Osnorio on January 16, 1940. Chamber president Juan Gonzalez (left) holds up the national flag of Mexico with help from Consul Osnoria. Also identified are, from left to right, Jose Solis, Andres Alvarez Sr., Hector de Pena, C. R. Gonzales, and unidentified. (Photograph by John Frederick "Doc" McGregor.)

Chapter 1437 of the United Daughters of the Confederacy gather for a meeting at the Princess Louise Hotel on September 12, 1940. The hotel, designed by architect William Ward Watkin, was built in 1927. The United Daughters of the Confederacy was responsible for erecting a monument to confederate soldiers located on the bluff overlooking downtown. (Photograph by John Frederick "Doc" McGregor.)

Bearing flags from both Mexico and the United States, this automobile with a LULAC banner on the front participates in a Defense Day Parade on December 20, 1941. The League of United Latin American Citizens is the oldest and largest continually active Latino political association in the country and the first nationwide Mexican American civil rights organization according to the Handbook of Texas Online. LULAC was founded on February 17, 1929, in Corpus Christi as a result of the rise of the Mexican American middle class in Texas and the resistance to discrimination.

Snow blankets the ground as a man walks along Lower Broadway near the Driscoll Hotel in January 1940. Snow came to the area for two days starting around January 19. Corpus Christi Cathedral, which was under construction at the time, is in the background. The cornerstone would be laid in March and the building dedicated in July. (Photograph by John Frederick "Doc" McGregor.)

The 1000 block of Leopard Street attracts shoppers, diners, and loiterers in this 1941 image. Businesses identified include Jalisco Restaurant, the Grande Café, and the Grande Theater. Leopard Street became one of the most important thoroughfares in Corpus Christi in the early part of the 20th century. Its significance has diminished with the construction of Interstate Highway 37 and the Crosstown Expressway.

The girls badminton team from Corpus Christi High School brandish their "racquets" in the 1940s. The racquets look more like table tennis paddles. Some of the girls identified are Minnie Falcon, Christine Aboud, and Gladys Heslep. (Photograph by John Frederick "Doc" McGregor.)

Two women wearing traditional Mexican dresses ride with two men in a convertible during the Defense Day Parade on December 20, 1941. The word on the front of the car appears to be *amicitia*, which connotes friendship. *Laelius de Amicitia* is a treatise authored by Roman statesman Marcus Tullius Cicero, who pondered the meaning of friendship following the death of a good friend. (Photograph by John Frederick "Doc" McGregor.)

El Patio Mexican Food, at 201 North Water Street, is seen here on August 4, 1943. Corpus Christi, like other Texas cities, is replete with restaurants serving Tex-Mex cuisine. Water Street once sat at the edge of Corpus Christi Bay. Efforts to protect the city from tidal surges caused by hurricanes led Corpus Christi to fill in part of the bay and build a seawall to protect the downtown area from flooding.

From the very beginning, safety played a large role in the operation of industrial facilities located near the Port of Corpus Christi. Southern Alkali Corporation (later Pittsburg Plate Glass) understood the need and organized an emergency team to prevent accidents from happening and to deal with crises. (Photograph by John Frederick "Doc" McGregor.)

Members of the Corpus Christi Police Department stand in front of the Palace Theater on April 3, 1943. The theater is showing *The Last Roundup of Clyde Barrow & Bonnie Parker*. (Photograph by John Frederick "Doc" McGregor.)

An aerial view, facing north, of the Alameda Place subdivision bordered by Alameda Street, Santa Fe Street, and Louisiana Boulevard is shown here in 1940. The Louisiana Parkway can be seen running along the top of the photograph; Menger Elementary School, at 2401 South Alameda, is at the top left corner; and the street running in front of it is Alameda.

This view from the bluff on June 5, 1941, shows downtown looking east. Structures identified on the back of the image include city hall, Citizens Industrial Bank, the Old Lichtenstein Building, State National Bank, the W. W. Jones Building, Nueces Hotel, the Texas Building, the Furman Building, and the Lovenskiold Building. The recently completed Shoreline Boulevard and the Peoples Street T-head are in the background. (Photograph by John Frederick "Doc" McGregor.)

This February 16, 1940, photograph shows the 400 block of Chaparral Street. Structures identified on this block include the Medical-Professional Building, Faust Café, the Medical Club, Lee's Cigar Store, the Chicago Restaurant, and Texas State Bank. (Photograph by John Frederick "Doc" McGregor.)

Adm. Chester W. Nimitz, a native of Fredericksburg who commanded U.S. forces in the Pacific during World War II, visited Corpus Christi on June 18, 1946, for an inspection of Naval Air Station Corpus Christi. He was greeted with a parade attended by thousands that became known as the Nimitz Day Parade. Nimitz's prediction that Naval Air Station Corpus Christi would always play an important role in naval aviation has so far been proven to be true.

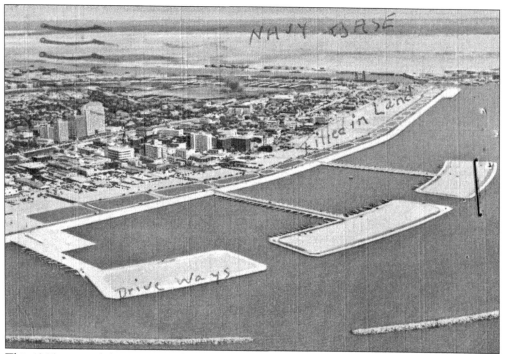

This 1945 postcard shows an aerial view of the Corpus Christi Yacht Basin not too long after the seawall, T-heads, and L-head were constructed. The person who sent the postcard, Fred Metts, pointed out the "driveways" around the outer rim of the L-head as well as the filled-in area that later became home to hotels and office buildings. The reference to the "Navy Base" is incorrect. Naval Air Station Corpus Christi is on the southern end of the city.

The Little Mexican Inn at 811 Leopard Street welcomes visitors to the city in a July 9, 1943, image. This part of Leopard Street was just a few blocks from the bluff overlooking downtown and Corpus Christi Bay. The area later became home to the uptown region of downtown Corpus Christi. (Photograph by John Frederick "Doc" McGregor.)

This aerial photograph taken in 1946 shows Corpus Christi as the small town it once was. Writing on the back refers to a new housing development near Santa Fe, Alameda, and Staples Streets. There are nothing but fields beginning at the bottom edge of the image in an area now packed with houses, businesses, and the highway known as South Padre Island Drive.

A float representing the Negro Chamber of Commerce was part of this Buccaneer Days Parade on June 8, 1940. The Cudd Food Store sign advertises meat, staples, and fancy groceries that included vegetables. It also boasts of "quality food and courteous service." The Negro Chamber of Commerce no longer exists under its original, or any other, name. There is, however, an Hispanic Chamber of Commerce. (Photograph by John Frederick "Doc" McGregor.)

Workers move part of the Church of the Good Shepherd, built in 1878 and located until 1949 at Chaparral and Taylor Streets, to Staples Street near Kostoryz Road (outside the city limits at that time) to become All Saints Episcopal Church. Moving what was known as "the little white church" occurred when Good Shepherd began building a new church. All Saints was admitted to the Diocese of West Texas a year later. It held its first service on February 19, 1949.

The Blue Angels performance team flies over the bay front sometime in the 1940s. Adm. Chester W. Nimitz ordered the formation of the team to showcase naval aviation. The Blue Angles performed its first demonstration flight less than a year later in June 1946. The team was based at Naval Air Station Corpus Christi from 1951 to 1954 and flew the F9F-5 while stationed here.

This 1950s photograph shows a man standing next to an old cotton gin machine. Cotton production in Nueces County hit its peak in the mid-1920s at more than 100,000 bales a year. Production fell in the 1930s and 1940s, with only 46,000 bales ginned in 1945. Cotton farming rebounded shortly thereafter, with more than 100,000 bales ginned in 1949. Since that time, cotton production has fallen as sorghum has become an increasingly important crop and taken over lands.

A Mexican Chamber of Commerce float is among those included in the Buccaneer Days Illuminated Night Parade in the 1950s. A man dressed as a Native American appears to be standing atop some sort of man-made mountain. The affiliation appears to be with a local chamber of commerce as opposed to one representing Mexico. This organization is now known as the Hispanic Chamber of Commerce.

People stand with hats off and heads bowed in what appears to be a benediction given at the June 17, 1950, opening of the Padre Island Causeway. The thoroughfare was later renamed the John F. Kennedy Memorial Causeway and, in recent years, was elevated to make hurricane evacuation easier. Before the causeway was raised, people risked being trapped on the island during a hurricane as high tides flooded the roadway. (Photograph by John Frederick "Doc" McGregor.)

The caption that accompanies this photograph reads, "Founder of the Ada Wilson Hospital of Physical Medicines and Rehabilitation for Crippled Children, talking to unidentified man." The unidentified man, as anyone familiar with Texas and U.S. history can attest, is Lyndon B. Johnson, who eventually became the 36th president of the United States. At the time this 1940s photograph was taken, Johnson was either a member of the U.S. House of Representatives, where he served six terms, or a member of the U.S. Senate, an office he won in 1948.

In this January 7, 1953, image, bus driver Juan Gonzales shows off one of the modern buses purchased by the Nueces Transportation Company to deliver passengers around town. Bus service is now handled by the Regional Transportation Authority, which was created by voters in 1985 to provide transportation to residents in Nueces and San Patricio counties.

Members of the Buccaneer Beard Club don pirate regalia and flout their beard-growing abilities. Pirates were known for their facial hair, and maybe the king of this club, seated on his throne atop a 1950s-era automobile, was chosen because of his ability to grow the longest, fullest beard.

Dr. Hector P. Garcia, seen here in 1958, was angered by the discrimination he saw aimed at Hispanic veterans and thus founded the American GI Forum in 1948 to improve veterans' benefits and enhance medical attention. It soon expanded to address educational and vocational training, housing, public education, voter registration, and other issues. Today the American GI Forum has nearly 160,000 members in 502 chapters in 24 states. Garcia is revered by many Corpus Christi residents.

Gabe Lozano Sr. (1909–1984) was the first Hispanic mayor of Corpus Christi. He was the son of Vicente Lozano, a pioneer merchant and a civic, education, and business leader. He was first elected to the city council in 1959 and served seven terms. He was the president of the League of United Latin American Citizens, a parks commissioner, and a director of the Corpus Christi Chamber of Commerce. His business interests included forming South Texas Telecasting Company and the International Radio Company, which operated station KCCT.

Directors of the Lower Nueces River Water Supply District pose after ground-breaking ceremonies for the Wesley E. Seale Dam in 1955. The state created the district to develop a larger water reservoir for Corpus Christi and South Texas. The dam, completed in 1958, is 1,000 feet downstream from the previous La Fruta Dam built in 1935. The dam is named for a former Corpus Christi mayor and chairman of the water supply district.

Construction of the Harbor Bridge began in June 1956 and was finished sometime in 1959. It opened to traffic on October 23, 1959, replacing the Bascule Bridge that had to be raised and lowered each time a ship or barge entered or left the Port of Corpus Christi's inner harbor. Construction of the Harbor Bridge began on each side of the Corpus Christi shipping channel and met in the middle. Four workers were killed during its construction.

Five

MODERN ERA GROWTH
1962–2000

The USS *Lexington*, now decommissioned and converted into a museum, was used to train numerous naval aviators stationed at Naval Air Station Corpus Christi in the delicate and life-threatening art of landing on an aircraft carrier. The *Lexington*, the most decorated aircraft carrier in World War II, was nicknamed "The Blue Ghost" after repeatedly defying reports that it had been sunk. The *Lexington* replaced the USS *Antietam* as an aviation-training carrier in the Gulf of Mexico in 1962. During the Cuban Missile Crisis, it resumed duties as an attack carrier, returning to its training mission in December 1963. Corpus Christi civic leaders campaigned to acquire the ship from the navy after it was announced the aircraft carrier would be decommissioned.

Corpus Christi resident Janet Grant feeds seagulls on one of the T-heads in the early 1960s. Seagulls are as much a part of the Corpus Christi "experience" as the water, wind, and beaches. Feeding them is allowed in most public places. Restaurants with outdoor seating, however, discourage the practice and construct intricate webs of fishing line above their patios to prevent the birds from swooping down and taking food from diners' plates. These aggressive birds have little fear of humans. If a person holds a piece of bread in an outstretched arm, a seagull will snatch it from his or her fingers.

Chief M. N. Schmidt dons a clown costume to entertain children at a Naval Air Station Kingsville Christmas party in 1963. The children are identified as Elena and Lucio Cortez, and the man on the right is Chief Petty Officer Dempsy. Naval air training fields in Corpus Christi, Beeville, and Kingsville provided training to thousands of naval aviators through the years. Chase Field in Beeville was closed but the other two remain in operation.

Ernest Borgman, chief park ranger at the Padre Island National Seashore, keeps an eye on the beaches, sand dunes, and wildlife that attract visitors to this vast expanse of undeveloped barrier island. Padre Island is 113 miles long (the longest barrier island in the nation), with 80 miles left in its natural state. White sand, grasslands, and saltwater marshes cover the island, and white-tailed deer, peregrine falcons, and coyotes call it their home. Pres. John F. Kennedy signed legislation to create the national seashore on September 28, 1962. Upon signing the bill, President Kennedy remarked, "[T]his measure will make possible a broad range of year-round opportunities for recreation and quiet enjoyment of a natural environment for a large number of people." The shrimp boat in the background ran ashore in 1963, providing a photogenic backdrop.

Bailey's Pharmacy at the intersection of Lexington Boulevard and Barton Drive in the Flour Bluff area of the city shared space with Little Mexico Tacos and Foodtown when this photograph was taken on February 6, 1964. The phone booth on the right is a relic of the past, rendered unnecessary by the age of cell phones. Flour Bluff, which is sometimes mistakenly referred to as a suburb rather than an area of Corpus Christi, has one of the best school districts in the area.

A group of women assemble dolls for the Navy Relief Christmas Drive in November 1964. The women are identified as Rosa Premo, Elizabeth Phillips, Blanche Buch, and Johnnie Hammond.

George H. W. Bush visited Corpus Christi in October 1964 while campaigning for the U.S. Senate. The future president was no stranger to Corpus Christi—he graduated from the third training class at Naval Air Station Corpus Christi in June 1943, becoming the youngest commissioned pilot in U.S. Navy history. Bush was elected to the U.S. House of Representatives twice but lost two bids for a Senate seat. After his second race for the Senate, President Nixon appointed him a delegate to the United Nations. He was elected president in 1988.

Santa Claus delivers presents to two unidentified boys from Boys City during a Naval Air Station Christmas party in 1964. The Optimist Club of Downtown Corpus Christi chartered Boys City in 1945. It opened its first home for neglected and abandoned boys a year later, and in 1955 a new facility opened near Driscoll on land donated by the Clara Driscoll Foundation. The Paul and Mary Haas Foundation donated funds in 1966 to expand facilities to include girls. In 1988, the Texas Education Agency and the Texas State Board of Education approved opening Coastal Bend Youth City Charter School.

Three cowboys get ready to head north for an annual trail ride to promote the San Antonio Livestock Show and Rodeo. The ride began at the J & J Dude Ranch in Corpus Christi and ended 140 miles later in Alamo City. The riders are identified as Jim Wight, Howard Stulting, and Howard Stulting Jr.

A group of Young Democrats gathers behind a table covered with posters touting the candidacy of Lyndon B. Johnson for president. LBJ was elected president after serving out the remainder of the term of John F. Kennedy. Texas, once a Democratic stronghold, gradually swung over to the Republican side. The Corpus Christi area, along with other South Texas cities, has remained Democratic, although Republicans have made significant inroads.

It did not take much room to hold a city council meeting in 1964. Members of the council are, from right to left, W. H. Wallace Jr., Jim Young, Dr. James L. Barnard, J. R. de Leon, M. P. Maldonado, and W. J. Roberts. The city government eventually left the downtown/bay front area for a new high-rise building on the corner of Leopard and Staples Streets.

Bishop M. S. Garriga lies in state at the Corpus Christi Cathedral after his death in 1965. He was appointed bishop in 1936 by Pope Pius XII and served until his death. The Corpus Christi Cathedral is one of the most architecturally significant structures in South Texas. Bishop Garriga consecrated the cathedral in 1952 and is entombed in the crypt chapel. After Garriga's death, the southern four counties of the Diocese were split off to form the new Diocese of Brownsville, with the former auxiliary bishop of Corpus Christi, Adolph Mark, serving as its bishop. On September 1, 1965, the Corpus Christi Diocese welcomed Garriga's replacement, Most Reverend Thomas J. Drury, who initiated renovation projects on the cathedral to comply with new liturgy promulgated by the Second Vatican Council.

Dr. George Garza, superintendent of schools of the West Oso Independent School District, and Gonzalo Campos, principal of Skinner Elementary School, walk outside the district's facilities in April 1965. West Oso education began with a one-room schoolhouse in 1884. Growing enrollment led to construction of a new building in 1916. West Oso serves students living in a northwestern section of Corpus Christi.

Workers fight a gas well blowout in the 1960s. Natural gas was first discovered in Nueces County in 1922. In San Patricio County alone, 37.9 million cubic feet of gas was produced by 1982. Oil and gas discoveries helped diversify the area's economy in the 1910s and 1920s, and in 1926, the first gas pipeline was laid from Refugio County gas fields to Aransas County.

Ernest Briones, who later served for many years as Nueces County clerk, visits with a young boy at a Nueces County Community Action Agency program in April 1965. The agency helps low-income residents by providing emergency food, assistance in finding rentals and with utility expenses, weatherization of homes, and other services.

Gudalia Saenz conducts a home-improvement demonstration during an adult Nueces County Community Action Agency program. The agency was created as part of the War on Poverty during Lyndon B. Johnson's presidency. Its mission was to work toward breaking the cycle of poverty by helping create a network of organizations to help the poor.

Three children work on a model boat float named SS *Liz* for a Buccaneer Days Junior Parade in the 1960s. The parade is held each year to give children an opportunity to participate in Buccaneer Days and be the stars of their own parade. The children are identified as, from left to right, Hector Mendieta, Becky Gonzales, and Ann Cooper.

A toll plaza at the entrance to the Padre Island Causeway, later renamed the John F. Kennedy Causeway, was set up to collect tolls to help pay for construction of the roadway connecting the mainland with Padre Island. The causeway had been open for more than a decade when this 1960s photograph was taken.

Fourteen members of the Feria de los Flores pose for a group picture in 1965. Members include Yolanda Medina, Gloria Garcia, Emily Garcia, and Laura Garza. The League of United Latin American Citizens created the pageant to give Hispanic women a chance to earn scholarships. Contestants apply for and are chosen to participate based on academics and community service. The contestants compete in categories that include dance, song, and personality. They wear glittery costumes and dance and sing to Folklorico music.

This is the intersection of Everhart Road and Lexington Boulevard (later changed to South Padre Island Drive) around 1965. The view appears to be taken from Everhart Road looking east. Lexington Boulevard was a divided thoroughfare at this time, but it was a far cry from the freeway that took its place.

Show animals like this female yearling are raised each year by students involved in agriculture education at their schools. The animals are then displayed and judged at county livestock shows, usually during the Christmas break from school. The animals are then auctioned off in order to provide scholarship money to the students. Some of the larger animals are sold for tens of thousands of dollars.

Mary Horn, a participant in the 1966 Feria de los Flores, displays a Folklorico dress chosen for this annual competition. Folklorico refers to traditional Latin American dances that emphasize local folk culture, and the dresses that are worn during these dances use the same name. Regions in Mexico, Central America, and the Southwestern United States are well known for Folklorico.

Ada Wilson, founder of Ada Wilson Hospital of Physical Medicine and Rehabilitation for Crippled Children, greets an unidentified child who was a patient at the hospital. They are joined by Lt. Col. Don Luce Lee M. Richardson, of Richardson Cotton Company, and Jimmie Rhodes, supervisor at what would eventually become known as the Corpus Christi Army Depot.

Corpus Christi Chamber of Commerce officers in 1965 included, from left to right, Glenn Lincoln, Richard King III, Preston Doughty, and R. N. Connolly. The chamber of commerce was born on February 15, 1924, with Henry B. Baldwin elected as the first president. It was originally located in a building on Starr Street before moving to the city council chambers of city hall, where it remained until 1940. It later moved to the fifth floor of the Nixon Building and in 1951 moved to its new headquarters at 1201 North Shoreline Boulevard.

A group of guests arrives at a barbecue given at the Armstrong Ranch's first production sale of Santa Gertrudis cattle. Pictured are Gus Wortham, Robert J. Kleberg Jr., Mrs. J. Deaver Alexander, and Sterling Evans. The Santa Gertrudis was developed by the King Ranch by breeding Brahman cattle with Shorthorn cattle. In 1940, the U.S. Department of Agriculture recognized the Santa Gertrudis as a purebred. The name Santa Gertrudis originates from Rincon de Santa Gertrudis, the original land grant purchased by Capt. Richard King, who established the first ranch headquarters there. This breed is known for its ability to resist heat and ticks as well as ease of calving, good mothering ability, and abundant milk production. They also have improved beef quality over most purebred Brahmans, and steers are noted for achieving high weight gains on both pasture and feedlots.

This 1966 photograph shows the Port of Corpus Christi and downtown Corpus Christi. The vessel nearest the south shore is a cargo ship outfitted with cranes to load freight on and off the ship. It is docked at one of the port's public cargo docks. These docks have since been torn down to make room for the Congressman Solomon P. Ortiz International Center and Whataburger Field. The international center is a popular meeting destination, and Whataburger Field is home to the Corpus Christi Hooks, a Double-A affiliate of the Houston Astros. Hall-of-Fame pitcher Nolan Ryan is the principal owner of the team.

Hurricane Beulah struck the Texas coast in September 1967. It was one of five severe hurricanes to affect the Texas middle coast in the 20th century. Corpus Christi avoided a direct hit from Beulah, which first came ashore in Brownsville before moving northward and making landfall at a point east of Alice. At landfall, winds near the center were measured at around 136 miles per hour.

Shrimp boats along the Coastal Bend were tossed around and wrecked by Hurricane Beulah in September 1967. Damage from winds and tides were heavy on Corpus Christi Beach and in the Aransas Pass and Rockport-Fulton areas. Most of the destruction from Beulah came from floods following heavy rains, which totaled 10 to 20 inches over a widespread area of Southern Texas and as many as 30 inches in some isolated areas.

Sand dunes are a unique element of South Texas terrain. Sand blowing off Gulf of Mexico beaches form dunes lining the eastern shores of Padre and Mustang Islands. These dunes nearest the water are known as "fore-island dunes." They form a natural dike, preventing storm tides from destroying grasslands. Sometimes gaps will form in the fore-island dunes that allow sand to blow out into the grasslands and produce other formations known as "blow-out dunes." Walking in the dunes is discouraged because paths created by walking can widen into large openings between dunes.

Construction on a new building for First United Methodist Church began on Shoreline Boulevard in the 1960s. In this photograph, two men work on the exterior of the chapel that sits atop a room now used by a local Boy Scout troop. FUMC is the oldest and largest Protestant church in the city. The Reverend John Hayne gave the first Methodist sermon in the city on February 8, 1846, during the months that Gen. Zachary Taylor (later U.S. president) camped on the shores of Corpus Christi Bay. Others in attendance were future general and U.S. president Ulysses S. Grant and future president of the American Confederacy, Jefferson Davis, both of whom served under Taylor.

Buccaneer Days pirate queen contestants (from left to right) Shirley Knetig, Linda Harris, and Sharon Fryer brandish their weapons (and a surfboard) on Padre Island before a 1960s contest. The contestants compete for the crown and scholarships. Each year, the pirate queens "kidnap" the mayor and force him or her to walk the plank off a sailboat into Corpus Christi Bay. Former mayor Mary Rhodes declined the invitation to be kidnapped, deferring the honor to former police chief and future mayor Henry Garrett.

James Polk (piano), Junior Alvarez (drums), Bobby Galvan (alto sax), Eddie Galvan (tenor sax), and Sam Galvan (bass) perform at the 1969 Corpus Christi Jazz Festival, an annual music festival still celebrated today. The Galvan family has a long history of playing in front of live audiences in the city.

Army helicopters like this are among the whirlybirds that employees of the Corpus Christi Army Depot (CCAD) see on a regular basis. CCAD overhauls, repairs, modifies, retrofits, tests, and modernizes engines and other components of helicopters for U.S. and foreign military customers. It began operations in 1961 as a small maintenance facility for fixed-wing aircraft and evolved into the army's largest helicopter repair, overhaul, and maintenance center.

This is Solomon M. Coles High School, at 924 Winnebago Street on the city's north side, as it appeared in the mid-1960s. It later became a middle school and then an elementary school before being closed down. It reopened in 2007 as Solomon Coles High School and Education Center.

Construction of a high bridge on the John F. Kennedy Causeway to carry automobile traffic above the Intracoastal Waterway (ICW) began in the 1970s. Before the bridge was completed, automobiles crossed to Padre Island via a drawbridge, which had to be raised or lowered whenever vessels traveling along the ICW came through the area. This allowed automobile and ship traffic to move more freely and improved the evacuation route from Padre Island. In the event of a hurricane, Padre Island can be evacuated in only two ways: the John F. Kennedy Causeway or the ferry system on the northern tip of Mustang Island to the north of Padre Island.

In this 1975 photograph, the Greenwood Branch Public Library Bookmobile cruised west side neighborhood streets to encourage residents to read. This branch of the Corpus Christi Public Library system specializes in bilingual and test preparation materials.

By 1977, the Nueces County Courthouse that was built in 1914 had begun the process of closing its doors as county officials moved into the new courthouse between Leopard and Lipan Streets. The courthouse has mostly sat in disrepair in the intervening years, with all sorts of proposals to refurbish it or tear it down. One ingenious city council member even proposed that the city contact Hollywood filmmakers and offer the structure as a prop in a movie in which it would be blown up. A grant in recent years funded restoration of one part of the courthouse, but it is still a long way from being brought back to its original state.

Hurricane Allen hit north of Brownsville in August 1980, bringing heavy rains and high winds to Corpus Christi. It made landfall as a Category 3 (out of 5) storm with sustained winds of 115 miles per hour. Here people wade in high water covering the road on the Lawrence Street T-head as storm debris blocks the entrance to the ramp.

An explosion at the Corpus Christi Public Grain Elevator, located on Port of Corpus Christi property, on April 7, 1981, led to the deaths of several people and injuries to two dozen more. Various theories as to the cause of the explosion led to much litigation. Reconstruction was completed in 1983, and the elevator was dedicated as the William E. Carl Terminal.

This is a view of Lake Corpus Christi looking west over the Wesley E. Seale Dam. The lake, which is owned by the City of Corpus Christi, has a storage capacity of 269,900 acre-feet. It is located 4 miles southwest of Mathis on the Nueces River and serves as a source of water for Corpus Christi. The earthen dam is 75 feet high. In 1934, the state leased 288 acres surrounding the lake from the city for a park.

Msgr. William C. Kinlough blesses the grave of Mr. and Mrs. Constancio H. Curiel, grandparents of Peggy Bryan, who is standing beside the monsignor in this November 2, 1982, photograph. The blessing came on Dia de los Muertos, a holiday celebrated in Mexico and by people of Mexican heritage living in the United States and Canada. It takes place on the first two days of November in connection with the Catholic holy days of All Saints' Day and All Souls' Day.

Different types of watercraft can be seen skimming across Corpus Christi Bay, the Laguna Madre, or the Gulf of Mexico. With warm weather almost year-round, the Coastal Bend is a great place to enjoy the water. Steady sea breezes make it an ideal spot for sailors and windsurfers. Bird Island Basin at the Padre Island National Seashore is a popular windsurfing site, attracting visitors from all over the world.

The Bayfront Plaza Convention Center opened in the 1980s to give Corpus Christi modern meeting and exhibition space. The center included an auditorium, exhibit space, and meeting rooms. In recent years, facilities have been expanded to include an auditorium large and modern enough to attract big-name performers. The facility sits on the northern end of Shoreline Boulevard overlooking Corpus Christi Bay.

Liz Pena talks to her friend Marlene Luna across her flooded front yard on Caroline Street. Corpus Christi receives about 30 inches of rain per year, and locals say it seems to fall all at once. Street flooding is common following a heavy rain, and extended periods of rainfall can lead to flooding along the Nueces River, forcing some to abandon their homes and leaving others stranded when floodwaters cover roadways.

Tony Bonilla (left), national president of the League of United Latin American Citizens, presents a certificate of new charter to LULAC Council 4387 of Robstown. Treasurer Rolando de Alejandro holds the certificate. The other man is identified as Israel S. Trevino. LULAC is one of two Hispanic civil-rights organizations founded in Corpus Christi.

Much of what comprises the Corpus Christi Bay can be seen in this 1980s aerial view of the bay front, T-heads, and L-head, including the Corpus Christi Yacht Club, the Lighthouse Restaurant, and plenty of slips occupied with pleasure boats. The twin towers of One Shoreline Plaza were added to the bay front in 1988.

Construction began at the current site of the Central Corpus Christi Library on September 8, 1984, at the corner of Comanche and Tancahua Streets. When the city made plans to move the main library the final time from Mesquite Street downtown to Comanche Street, they decided not to keep the La Retama name that had always been used for the library. It was located on Mesquite Street from 1955 to 1986. A ribbon-cutting for the new library was held on June 10, 1986.

J. C. Penny was among several retailers that shuttered their businesses in downtown Corpus Christi. Downtown windows were covered with plywood to prevent vandals from breaking windows, and the Downtown Management District began working to revitalize the area. The effort has been difficult, but some progress has been made. Bars, nightclubs, and restaurants are now more common than they have been in the past, and efforts to turn old buildings into urban living spaces are in the works.

James B. McCullough served as Corpus Christi postmaster from February 6, 1982, to November 30, 1990. William Aubrey served as the city's first postmaster, beginning work in May 1946 when the first post office was established in the city. In 1908, a post office was established in the Calallen area and remained open until 1965.

Books like these would be almost impossible to produce had it not been for the work of John Frederick "Doc" McGregor, who took thousands of photographs between the 1930s and the 1950s. McGregor was not a professional photographer and earned a living as a chiropractor, but he took it upon himself to chronicle much of Corpus Christi's history and culture after moving here with his family in 1929. Whether he intended it or not, McGregor became one of the city's greatest historians. His photographs can be viewed online at the Corpus Christi Public Library Web site, www.library.ci.corpus-christi.tx.us. He is shown here outside First United Methodist Church in what may be the last photograph ever taken of him. The image was taken by his friend Margaret Ramage.

Visit us at
arcadiapublishing.com